MICROBE WARS

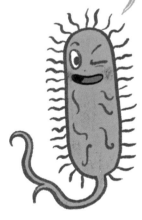

This book is dedicated to all the scientists — from lab technicians to professors — working to increase our knowledge of microbes and helping us fight the Microbe Wars.
— GA

For my favourite mikrobio: *Alex.*
— MM

A TEMPLAR BOOK

First published in the UK in 2021 by Templar Books,
an imprint of Bonnier Books UK,
The Plaza, 535 King's Road, London, SW10 0SZ
Owned by Bonnier Books,
Sveavägen 56, Stockholm, Sweden
www.bonnierbooks.co.uk

ISBN 978-1-78741-915-5

This book was typeset in Quasimoda,
Acier BAT, Goodlife, and Bowman
The illustrations were created digitally

Edited by Katie Haworth and Samuel Fern
Designed by Nathalie Eyraud
Production by Neil Randles

Printed in Poland

MICROBE WARS

Written by Gill Arbuthnott

Illustrated by Marianna Madriz

templar
books

A NOTE FROM GILL

I love microbes. They've fascinated me since I first met them when I was studying Biology at university and I've enjoyed passing on what I've learned to hundreds of school pupils during my time in teaching and seeing many of them become fascinated in turn.

I'm sure many more people are aware of the importance of microbes now than was the case at the end of 2019, but this book hasn't been written as a response to the COVID-19 pandemic. I'll have failed if you finish reading and think of microbes as nasty germs that make you ill. The overwhelming majority do us no harm and many are useful or even vital to us. But this book isn't just about microbes. It's about the scientists and doctors who discovered how important they are, who developed disinfectants and antibiotics and vaccines to help us fight the Microbe Wars. I hope by the time you finish reading, you'll be a fan of microbes too!

A NOTE FROM MARIANNA

Illustrating a book about microbes in the middle of a global pandemic was quite a unique experience. Gill's imaginative stories and inquisitive characters provided me with many rich challenges, and plenty of laugh-out-loud moments — which were especially important during some dark times.

I had so much fun giving these heroes, villains, humans and microbes the energy and personalities inspired by the many cartoons I loved watching after school. I hope they have the power to capture your attention, absorb you fully into their universes, and make you have a fun time in the process!

CONTENTS

THE INVISIBLE WORLD

There's a whole world of microbes, too tiny to see. And they're not just around us...

...they're on us and inside us too!

You can probably name some of history's deadliest diseases, but do you know what caused them? What they did? Where they went?

The Black Death killed 30 per cent of Europe's population, but was it really the rats, or did they just get bad press? Why did COVID-19 cause worldwide mayhem? Is the age of antibiotics ending, and how might wallabies save us?

Not all microbes are harmful. In fact, most are helpful, or even vital. They can make beer and wine, delicious foods, life-saving drugs and work day and night deep in our guts to keep our bodies healthy.

You probably don't know what your microbiome is yet, but you'll be amazed at the world you never knew you were protecting, and the trillions of little life forms depending on you!

Whether it's humans against microbes, microbes against microbes or humans fighting each other *with* microbes, our planet has been the battlefield of the Microbe Wars since life first began. Now it's time for you to join in!

MICROSCOPIC MARVELS

Nobody knew these tiny organisms existed, until the invention of the microscope...

FIRST CONTACT

The first person to see microbes was Dutchman **Antoni van Leeuwenhoek** (1632–1723).

At the time, most microscope lenses could only make something look 20–30 times bigger, but Van Leewenhoek's special lens could magnify it 260 times!

He was amazed when it revealed what he called 'animalcules' whizzing around in a drop of pond water...

Good grief! There's something waving at me!

I might be small, but I can take you!

I'm the elephant of the microbe world!

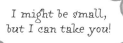

Virus   Bacterium   Protist

HOW SMALL IS TINY?

There are four microbe groups: **protists**, **fungi**, **bacteria** and **viruses**. They're vastly different sizes, but what does that even mean? Well, if a protist was the size of an elephant, a bacterium would be as small as a rabbit and a virus would be like a mouse!

We often measure things in centimetres or millimetres, but protists and bacteria are so small we measure them in micrometres. There are 1,000 micrometres in 1 millimetre, and most bacteria are only a few micrometres long.

But that's nothing compared to viruses. Viruses are so small that we have to use nanometres. There are 1,000 nanometres in 1 micrometre, so that's 1,000,000 nanometres in just 1 millimetre — and some viruses are only 20 nanometres wide!

Still surprised you can't see them? Well, now we know where to look, it's time to say hello!

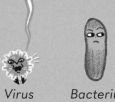

Squeak!

MEET THE MICROBES

There are roughly a trillion (1,000,000,000,000) species of microbe, most of them still unknown. And just because they are all small, that doesn't mean they are all similar: a **yeast** cell has more in common with a human than a bacterium. Give it up for protists and fungi!

PROTISTS

Protists are found in seawater, soil and fresh water. **Protozoa** are like tiny animals, while **algae** are more like plants. If you look at a drop of pond water under a microscope you can see loads of protozoa zipping around. Although each one is only a single cell, they all look very different.

I'm Paramecium and I'm a protozoan too. I whizz through the water spinning as I go, because the little 'hairs' on my body act like tiny oars. Just as well I don't get dizzy easily!

I'm a protozoan called **Amoeba**. I look like a fried egg and creep around in ponds by changing shape.

Navicula's the name, and me and my friends make lots of the oxygen that you breathe. We're a pretty big deal.

DIVING DIATOMS

Diatoms are single-celled algae which make their own food by using energy in sunlight to turn water and carbon dioxide into glucose (sugar). That's **photosynthesis**!

They're protected by tiny, beautiful shells of transparent silica, and these shells can last for millions of years underwater.

Diatom shells are used in products like toothpaste, soap and skin cleansers, in swimming pool filters and as insecticides. Living diatoms produce at least 20 percent of the oxygen we breathe.

FUNGI

Fungi aren't all microbes — you don't need a microscope to find mushrooms in the supermarket — but many fungi are single-celled and microscopic.

Fungi feed by releasing liquid that breaks down the cells of nearby **organisms** into simple substances like sugars and amino acids. The fungi use them to make new cells. This is helpful if the fungi are breaking down something dead that you want to decay — a compost heap, for instance — but they're not all good news. Some fungi love to snack on your food (potato blight) or even your feet (athlete's foot)!

Hi there! I'm *Fusarium venenatum*. I know I'm not much to look at, but I'm very tasty. I make a meat substitute called Quorn.

I'm a bread mould; bakeries hate me!

Really?

Oh yes, I'll eat any loaf!

Wholemeal or white, we don't mind!

Woe is me, I have the blight!

Heh, heh, heh... I'm Phytophthora, the potato blight fungus. You might like to mash or roast them, but I only ROT them!

THE GIANT AMONG US

Although most fungi are tiny, one may be the largest organism on Earth! A honey fungus nicknamed *the humongous fungus* which lives in Oregon, US, is about 3.8 kilometres across — mostly underground!

MEET MORE MICROBES

You didn't think that was all of them, did you? The show goes on! These are the real A-Listers; you've probably heard about some before, or seen others on TV. But you wouldn't want to see them *all* performing live...

BACTERIA

All the world's a stage for bacteria: these single cells are found almost everywhere, including your skin and guts! In fact, you have at least as many bacteria cells in your body as human cells — so who's really in charge? Some bacteria make their own food, while many feed like fungi. Luckily, most bacteria are harmless or even super helpful, but others live as parasites in other living things and these can cause diseases like sore throats and food poisoning.

Help is at hand! I'm **Bifidobacterium** and I'm a hero. I live in your gut and fight off invaders like Clostridium. Biff! Pow!

Everyone loves a villain, and I'm the worst of all! I'm *Clostridium botulinum* and I could end the world! But I probably won't.

HIYAH!

HERO OR VILLAIN?

Clostridium botulinum bacteria live in soil, but occasionally gets into damaged tins of food. This bacteria makes the most toxic substance of any living thing – botulinum **toxin**. Less than 100 grams of it could kill everyone in the world, and people inject it into their faces! If you make it very dilute, it's called Botox and smooths out skin wrinkles, and can also help patients with chronic pain.

VIRUSES

Viruses aren't alive. They aren't even cells. They're just bits of **DNA** or **RNA** with instructions for making — you guessed it — more viruses, all wrapped up in protein and sometimes fat. They hijack cells, breaking in and making them produce more viruses. This damages the cells and causes diseases like flu and COVID-19. Viruses attack every living thing: even bacteria!

I'm avian influenza, the bird flu virus, and I'm always lurking in the wings!

I can pass between birds easily but I'm no good at infecting humans yet. Scientists are keeping an eye on me — and I love an audience!

I hope they throw these after the show!

I'm Potyvirus, the tulip breaking virus. I can really ruin them, but I also give them amazing stripy flowers!

THE INVISIBLE THREAT

Although people have known since 1898 that viruses exist, they are so small that you can't see them with an ordinary microscope, which shines light through glass lenses. It wasn't until the invention of the powerful electron microscope in the 1930s that scientists saw a virus for the first time.

THE BLACK DEATH

You've probably heard of the plague, one of the scariest sicknesses in human history, but do you know the full story?

In 1347, trading ships arrived in Sicily. Many of the sailors were dead or dying. The 'death ships' had brought Black Death (sometimes called plague) from Asia to Europe. It killed between a quarter and a third of Europe's population, then went very quiet from 1770.

When you sang 'Ring a ring o' roses', I bet you didn't know you were singing about *that*! The 'ring o' roses' rash and '*atishoo*' sneezing were early symptoms. The '*pocket full of posies*' was because people thought sniffing a bunch of flowers or herbs would protect them (it didn't).

LONDON BURNING!

The Great Fire of London in 1665 began in a bakery in Pudding Lane, in the midst of a plague outbreak that had killed one in seven Londoners. The flames destroyed most of the city, but it did destroy enough of the germs to end the wave of sickness.

SIGNS & SYMPTOMS

The disease sometimes started with the rash and sneezing, then you would develop painful lumps called **buboes** in your armpits and groin and purple spots on your skin. The lumps, which were full of bacteria, turned black (hence the name) and if they burst, you were doomed…

16

This is God's anger! You have sinned too much and prayed too little.

SMELLS, SPELLS & SPECULATION

In medieval Europe, nobody knew about microbes. So when they were struck with diseases for no clear reason, they looked for answers in religion and superstition. Here are some theories of the day...

I'm a good man, so it won't harm me. Just to make sure, I will donate this image of St. Sebastian to the church.

They say in London that wearing sapphires or amber will prevent this illness. Rich people are always right!

My friends told me it's caused by witches, so we're going to burn down Granny Ogg's cottage to stop her evil ways. I've never liked Ogg.

BUT WHAT REALLY CAUSED IT?

We're not absolutely sure, even now. Most scientists think it was caused by bacteria carried by fleas which live on rats. It's still around today and causes a disease called bubonic plague, but we can treat it now with **antibiotics**.

Other scientists think Black Death was caused by a virus that died out completely when Black Death vanished in the 17th century. If a virus kills almost everyone it infects, in the end it runs out of places to reproduce and fizzles out.

I've heard that bad smells cause it. If I smell this posy of sweet herbs, it might protect me.

They're all idiots. It's you, the fleas!

It's not us, it's the bacteria! You need to learn some science.

Wear this around your neck. It's powdered toad, mixed with toad vomit. Trust me.

THE PLAGUE VILLAGE

In September 1665, fleas in a bale of cloth that had been sent to the Derbyshire village of Eyam from London started to bite people. Those people started to die of plague.

Somehow, the village rector, William Mompesson, persuaded most of the villagers to quarantine themselves, so they wouldn't spread plague to other towns. No one went in or out of Eyam. By November 1666, when the outbreak ended, 260 villagers had died, out of a population of fewer than 800, but their sacrifice had saved hundreds of other people.

PLAGUE!

NO ENTRY

DISEASES THAT SHOOK THE WORLD

The Black Death is long gone now, but many diseases have troubled us just as badly throughout human history. Let's meet three of the very worst...

SMALLPOX: SPOTS & SCARS

You won't ever have met a smallpox victim. This virus is the only disease that humans have managed to totally wipe out.

Be very glad it's gone. If you caught it, you came out in terrible spots and a fever. It killed three in every ten people who had it, and if you survived you would be marked with awful scars.

In Europe in the 17th and 18th centuries, it was fashionable to cover these smallpox scars with patches of black velvet on your face if you were rich – or mouse skin if you were poor!

Smallpox also spread very easily. When the Europeans invaded South America, they brought it with them. Smallpox may have devastated the Aztec and Incan empires.

(Find out how we beat smallpox on p. 28.)

Hmmph! Thanks for painting the scars.

I changed the face of history!

FAMOUS FACES OF SMALLPOX

Scientists found evidence I'd died of smallpox on my mummified body.

PHAROAH RAMSES V

I wore white lead makeup to cover the scars.

QUEEN ELIZABETH I

Smallpox struck me just after my most famous speech, the Gettysburg Address.

PRESIDENT LINCOLN

SPANISH FLU: A WAR BETWEEN WARS

Usually influenza makes you feel rotten, but it won't kill you. Spanish flu was different. It appeared across the globe in 1918, near the end of the First World War. We're not sure where it started, but despite the name, it probably wasn't Spain. Most types of flu appear first in animals in Asia, then infect humans.

I killed 50 million people in 18 months — more than the First World War.

The most dangerous flu viruses live in birds like ducks. We're not as safe as we seem!

Pigs can catch bird flu, and we act as a mixing bowl for it to change enough to infect humans. We might have caused the outbreak of Spanish flu.

Spanish flu tended to kill young, fit people, which made it even worse. We think that was because their immune systems (see p. 30) overreacted and attacked their own organs.

(see p. 30)

Famous animator Walt Disney caught Spanish Flu at 16.

The world will never see my work now! The name 'Walt Disney' will be forgotten...

Luckily, he pulled through!

MALARIA: THE MOSQUITO MALADY

Malaria is caused by a protist in mosquito saliva. When an infected mosquito bites someone, it passes the infectious protist along.

Malaria was common in ancient Egypt and the Roman Empire, and persisted in Europe and North America until the mid-20th century. It was treated with wormwood in ancient China and the bark of the cinchona tree in Peru. Drugs from these plants are still used now.

Today it's only found in tropical areas, but even in 2018 there were still 228 million cases and 405,000 deaths worldwide. The best way to prevent malaria is to use mosquito nets and repellents so they can't bite you in the first place.

We female mosquitos bite you to get blood protein for our eggs. Males don't bite; they only eat nectar.

Malum insectum!

Ooh, a tasty Roman. My baby protists might learn Latin!

When a French general in Macedonia in the First World War was ordered to attack, he sent the following reply:

URGENT

Regret that my army is in hospital with malaria

COVID-19

In 2019, no one had ever heard of COVID-19, but in 2020 it shook the world and we are still dealing with its effects. It isn't as infectious as smallpox or as deadly as the Black Death and scientists have worked incredibly hard to suppress it, but many people have lost someone they love to COVID-19.

WHAT IS IT?

COVID-19 is the disease caused by a virus which scientists have named SARS-CoV-2. It belongs to a group of viruses called **coronaviruses**, named for the spikes that stick out of their surface, which look a bit like the points on a crown.

There are lots of different coronaviruses, each with their own scientific name. Some of them cause mild diseases like the common cold, but others, like COVID-19, SARS and MERS are more serious.

WHERE DID IT COME FROM?

COVID-19 was first reported in Wuhan, China and spread rapidly across the world, largely due to air travel. Bats carry lots of coronaviruses and many scientists think one of their viruses changed in a way that allowed it to infect humans (and other mammals) but we may never know the full story.

HOW DOES IT AFFECT PEOPLE?

The most common symptoms are a cough, a fever and changes to your sense of taste or smell. Other symptoms include headaches, muscle aches, tiredness, sore throat and stomach upsets. It can severely affect breathing, and cause respiratory issues that put some patients on ventilators.

We're not sure why symptoms vary so much, or why some people don't even notice they're infected, and that makes it hard to control. Most people recover in days, others might take months, and it can hospitalise or even be fatal to some.

WHAT ARE WE DOING ABOUT IT?

Scientists have developed **vaccines** for it in record time, but these have gone through the same tests and safety checks as any other vaccine.

In January 2020, as soon as they heard about the outbreak in Wuhan, two Turkish scientists in Germany, Uğur Şahin and Özlem Türeci, began to develop a vaccine at their company BioNTech. A team at Oxford University, led by Professor Sarah Gilbert, also began work on a vaccine, as did many others. They needed the facilities to be able to make huge quantities as soon as possible, so BioNTech partnered with the Pfizer company, and Oxford with AstraZeneca. Over the next year, many of the trial vaccines failed, but in December 2020, the Pfizer-BioNTech vaccine was approved, followed shortly by the Oxford-AstraZeneca vaccine. Even mor vaccines have since been approved in 2021.

Scientists can also make monoclonal antibodies, which are proteins grown in laboratories, and these can be used to treat COVID-19 patients.

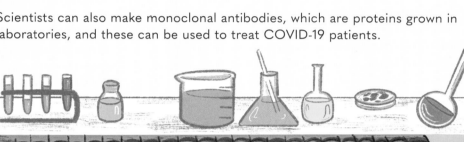

HOW CAN WE PROTECT EACH OTHER?

Some of the methods we've used to deal with COVID-19 have been around for centuries: self-isolation is just another word for **quarantine**. 'Contact tracing' works out who has been near other people to see how the disease might spread. Social distancing means staying too far away from each other for the virus to travel in coughs or sneezes. Hand washing, masks and other types of PPE (Personal Protective Equipment) help prevent infections by stopping the virus entering or escaping your body.

WHAT DOES THE FUTURE HOLD?

Viruses change over time, often becoming more infectious but less dangerous. COVID-19 is unlikely to disappear, but if enough people get **immunised**, it's much harder for the virus to spread. By controlling the spread, we should have enough time to adjust our vaccines as the virus **mutates** into slightly different versions.

We should have more drugs to treat its effects and make deaths much rarer. Beyond COVID-19, we will be more generally aware of how viruses spread and how basic precautions like hand washing can help: already we've seen flu **infections** plummet because of anti-COVID precautions. Perhaps, as people already do in many Asian countries, it might become common for everyone to wear masks for mild illnesses as well. Life *will* get back to normal, even though COVID-19 may still be around.

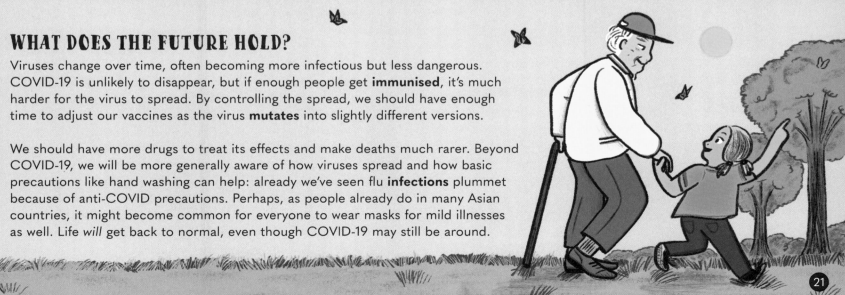

PREVENTING PANDEMICS

In the last hundred years, there have been outbreaks of new diseases which could have gone on to be pandemics and cause great loss of life.
Few made the jump from epidemic to pandemic, but why?
How have we managed to control them?

PANDEMIC FACTORS

To be classed as a pandemic, scientists consider how easily the disease spreads, how long before symptoms are visible in someone infectious, whether a vaccine and treatments can be developed, and the fatality rate: the percentage of infected people who die.

You can go far travelling by handshakes!

EBOLA

Ebola fever has a death rate of 50 per cent and can spread from animals to people. The symptoms include fever, vomiting, internal bleeding and liver and kidney failure.

Since the first outbreak in 1976, there have been Ebola epidemics in West Africa, but not a pandemic. This may be because someone with Ebola isn't infectious until they show symptoms, and it spreads by contact with body fluids or by touch, and not through coughs and sneezes. There are tests to identify Ebola, drugs to treat it and two vaccines.

Not many diseases have spread as widely as I have.

Have you heard them blaming the pigs?

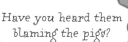

SWINE FLU

Swine flu was first seen in Mexico in 2009. Despite its name, humans probably gave it to the pigs! Symptoms include chills, aches, and fever.

Swine flu spread rapidly through coughs and sneezes among young people. Thankfully, the death rate was no higher than normal flu (about 0.1 per cent) and symptoms were usually mild. Swine flu is now seasonal, circulating every winter, and many people have some level of immunity.

HUMAN IMMUNODEFICIENCY VIRUS

HIV was first recognised in the 1980s, and has killed around 33 million people worldwide. HIV weakens the immune system, making it difficult for people to fight other infections such as pneumonia. It spreads via blood and bodily fluids, including breast milk.

At first, there were no treatments, but there is now a range of drugs which can prevent infection and help infected people stay healthy. Infection and death rates are falling, but roughly 38 million people are estimated to still be living with HIV.

SEVERE ACUTE RESPIRATORY SYNDROME (SARS)

SARS is an airborne coronavirus with a 14 per cent fatality rate. It first appeared in China in 2002, and it causes fever, muscle pains and breathing difficulties.

SARS spreads by coughs and sneezes or by touch. There is no cure or vaccine, so controlling it depends on contact tracing, quarantine, hand-washing and protective clothing. Because it only spreads from people with symptoms, it was possible to control it quickly. There have been no cases since 2004.

MIDDLE-EASTERN RESPIRATORY SYNDROME (MERS)

MERS is also caused by a coronavirus, and originated in Saudi Arabia in 2012. Similar to SARS, MERS causes a fever, cough and severe breathing difficulties, with a 35 per cent fatality rate. The virus started in camels before passing to humans, but we don't know how.

It needs close contact to pass between people, so most cases have been healthcare workers infected by their patients. There are no treatments or vaccines.

AVIAN FLU

Avian flu or 'bird flu' is common in chickens and ducks in certain countries. If it passes to humans, it carries a high death rate. Early symptoms include a fever, muscle aches and a cough, which can develop into pneumonia and severe breathing difficulties, but we have antivirals to help treat it.

In 1997, scientists in Hong Kong had to kill millions of potentially infected birds to stop an outbreak from becoming a lethal pandemic. Small outbreaks have happened since, but mostly from birds infecting humans. It can't pass easily between us yet, but organisations like the WHO (World Health Organisation) include avian flu in their pandemic planning.

GERM WARFARE

Unhappily, not every human has seen the destructive power of microbes as a bad thing. Throughout the years, our species has done some pretty awful things to weaponise their grisly effects...

BIOLOGICAL BATTLEFIELDS

Using microbes as weapons is known as germ warfare. Because microbes can spread beyond the battlefield to hurt civilians, it was widely banned in 1972. You might think the idea sounds modern, but armies have weaponised microbes for millenia.

For instance, ancient Roman soldiers would put rotten animals into enemy wells to poison their water supplies.

In 1346 an army in Russia threw the bodies of Black Death victims over city walls to infect the people inside.

Black Death

Death is my second name!

I'll outlast you by centuries!

Malaria

In the 1800s, Napoleon Bonaparte's French army, fighting the British, flooded their battlefield to help breed malarial mosquitoes. Over 100 British soldiers died fighting, but 4,000 died of disease.

We must oppose the English with nothing but fever, which will soon devour them all!

Remember: bite the British first, and save the French for dessert!

THE SCOTTISH SHEEP SACRIFICE

In 1942, British scientists transported sheep to a Scottish island called Gruinard, then blew up a small bomb near them. None of the sheep were hurt in the blast, yet a few days later, every single one was dead. But how?

The bomb was filled with anthrax bacteria, and the scientists were testing it on sheep so they could use it against humans in the Second World War. Anthrax is really nasty because the bacteria can form **spores** (like tiny seeds) which can survive in soil for decades, potentially hundreds of years.

Anthrax was never used in the Second World War. But what happened to Gruinard and all those spores?

Those sheep think they're on holiday, but they've had the wool pulled over their eyes.

Wait until they meet us!

Anthrax bacteria

CAUTION

POISON!

They covered the shore with barbed wire and warnings, and no one could go there for almost 40 years.

In 1986 scientists sprayed chemicals to kill the spores and destroyed tons of soil. They left more sheep to show it was safe, and in 1990 the wire and warnings were taken down.

I know it's technically safe, but let's just go to Greece instead.

200 YEARS OF HIDE & SEEK

A WEIS DECISION

Before the mid-19th century, no one knew what caused infections like sepsis (blood poisoning from bacteria), so no one knew how to prevent them. This made hospitals incredibly dangerous. Doctors carrying out operations just wore their normal clothes, maybe an apron to catch bloodstains, walked from patient to patient and stuck their dirty hands straight in!

In 1847 a Hungarian doctor, Ignaz Semmelweis, started making medical students wash their hands after examining corpses. The death rate from infections in his hospital dropped from eighteen percent to one percent, but it still didn't catch on. Finally, in 1864 a French scientist, Louis Pasteur, proved that bacteria and viruses caused infections, and hospitals finally turned hygienic! You'll hear more about him in a minute...

SNOW VS. WATER

In the 19th century, people thought cholera was caused by miasma (bad air). But when John Snow (1813–1858) traced an outbreak in London to a public water pump, he found evidence that microbes in the water were behind it all! When the pump was closed, cholera cases fell sharply.

NOTHING GETS PAST PASTEUR

Louis Pasteur (1822–95) studied **fermentation** (the process that produces wine — see p. 43) and why wine spoiled, and he believed that it was all down to microbes. He discovered you could avoid wine spoiling by heating it up between 60 and 100 degrees Celsius, killing the microbes off! Nowadays **pasteurisation** is used worldwide to destroy microbes in milk, fruit juice and beer.

But how did he prove Semmelweis right? Well, Pasteur also developed vaccines which would only have worked if Semmelweis's theories were correct. In 1881 he developed one against anthrax bacteria, and in 1885 he was working on one against the rabies virus, and tested it when nine-year-old Joseph Meister faced certain death after being mauled by a rabid dog. Luckily, the vaccine worked, saving Joseph's life.

Eurgh, why do the humans always win?

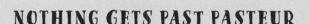

It's okay, we'll only start chopping when you start napping.

You guys have washed that needle, right?

Quick, jab him!

LISTER'S LAST RESORT

Even with basic hygiene and **anaesthetics**, surgery was very risky. Surgeon Joseph Lister (1827–1912) knew about Pasteur's work and finally went to war with microbes, cleaning surgical instruments, wounds, and even surgeons' hands with carbolic acid. Lister's **antisepsis** system has saved countless lives.

Now surgery is carried out in **aseptic** conditions, by cleaning the room with **antiseptics**, filtering the air, heating up surgical instruments — and always washing hands!

FAR-FLUNG FRIEDMANN

Roseli Ocampo-Friedmann (1937–2005) was a Filipino-American scientist who wanted to find out how tough microbes are, and the extreme conditions they might be able to endure. She discovered microbes in areas presumed to be totally lifeless like the deserts of Antarctica, where Friedmann Peak has been named in her honour. Her work has even been used by NASA to theorise about microbes on Mars!

EDWARD JENNER & VACCINATION

In Turkey in 1717, English writer Lady Mary Wortley Montagu (1689–1762) saw locals protect their children against smallpox by variolation: scraping out the **pus** of a smallpox blister, then scratching someone else's skin and poking the pus inside to give them a milder form of the deadly disease. Lady Mary had her son **inoculated** in Turkey, then introduced the treatment to England.

> Smallpox took my beauty. It will not take my children.

In 1757 a small boy called Edward Jenner was inoculated...

> Ouch!

Edward Jenner grew up to be a country doctor, at a time when superstitions said that milk-maids couldn't catch smallpox. However, he noticed they often caught the milder *cowpox* while at work.

> Morning, Sarah! Hi, Blossom!

> Morning, Dr Jenner!

Jenner thought cowpox might give protection against smallpox and in 1796 he planned to find out. But this wasn't just any experiment: if he failed, he would be hanged for murder!

> We both look very alike...

> ...and we both give you spots full of pus.

> But I'm good, or only a little bit bad...

> ...and I'm surely the worst of us!

cowpox

smallpox

Dr Jenner's gardener had an eight-year-old son named James Phipps, and Jenner persuaded the family to let him experiment on James. (This would never be allowed to happen nowadays, so don't worry!)

> Ow!

> Oh, I really don't want to hurt him!

Jenner took pus from a milk-maid's cowpox spot, scratched James' skin and rubbed the pus in. James got cowpox, but soon recovered.

Six weeks later, Jenner scratched James' arm again, and (risking both their lives) put smallpox pus inside.

Ouch!

Cowpox? You've got no chance!

Try it, Smallpox!

Jenner waited...

If Jenner was right, cowpox would protect James from smallpox. But if Jenner was wrong, James might die — and his death would send Jenner to the gallows.

James, how are you feeling?

Fine thanks.

Sniffles? Sneezes? One little spot?

Nope, all good.

Luckily for them both, Jenner really had found a way to immunise people against smallpox: James never got sick!

But...how? I've killed thousands! You're just... eurgh...

I am the champion!

Jenner called this method vaccination, because in Latin, the word 'vacca' means cow. Vaccination was much safer than variolation.

Jenner vaccinated more children, including his own baby, but the public didn't understand the science, and that made them suspicious and angry. There's a famous cartoon from the time showing people turning into cows after vaccination!

But as more and more people saw vaccination working, they praised Jenner for his genius.

In 1967 the WHO decided to exterminate smallpox worldwide, and in 1980 they succeeded.

I'm the last sample left, all locked up so they can make a vaccine out of me if anyone catches it again. That darn Jenner ruined me!

DANGER!

BEWARE!

So that's how vaccines came around, but what actually happens inside the body? Time to visit the real battlefield...

YOUR IMMUNE SYSTEM

Your skin stops most microbes from getting into your body, but what about the sneaky ones that creep into your mouth and nose to get at your guts and lungs? What catches those?

ALL IN A DAY'S BLOODWORK

In your bloodstream, there are red and white blood cells. White blood cells are part of your immune system, and they're split into two groups: **phagocytes** and **lymphocytes**.

Meanwhile, red blood cells carry oxygen around the body for your cells.

> I'm a red blood cell. We give your blood its colour!

> I'm a phagocyte, and I move out of blood vessels to destroy bacteria and viruses in the body.

> I'm a lymphocyte. I make chemicals called antibodies that make bacteria and viruses easier for my phagocyte friends to eat.

ON THE LOOKOUT

All cells, including bacteria, have markers called **antigens** that stick out of their surface. Every cell in your body has antigens that identify it as part of you, like passports, so your immune system knows they're allowed to be there.

> There are lots of different lymphocytes. We each make a different antibody to fit each bad antigen, like puzzle pieces. We lock in for battle!

Anything that isn't part of you, like a virus or nasty bacteria, has antigens too. Your immune system watches out for them, and attacks on sight!

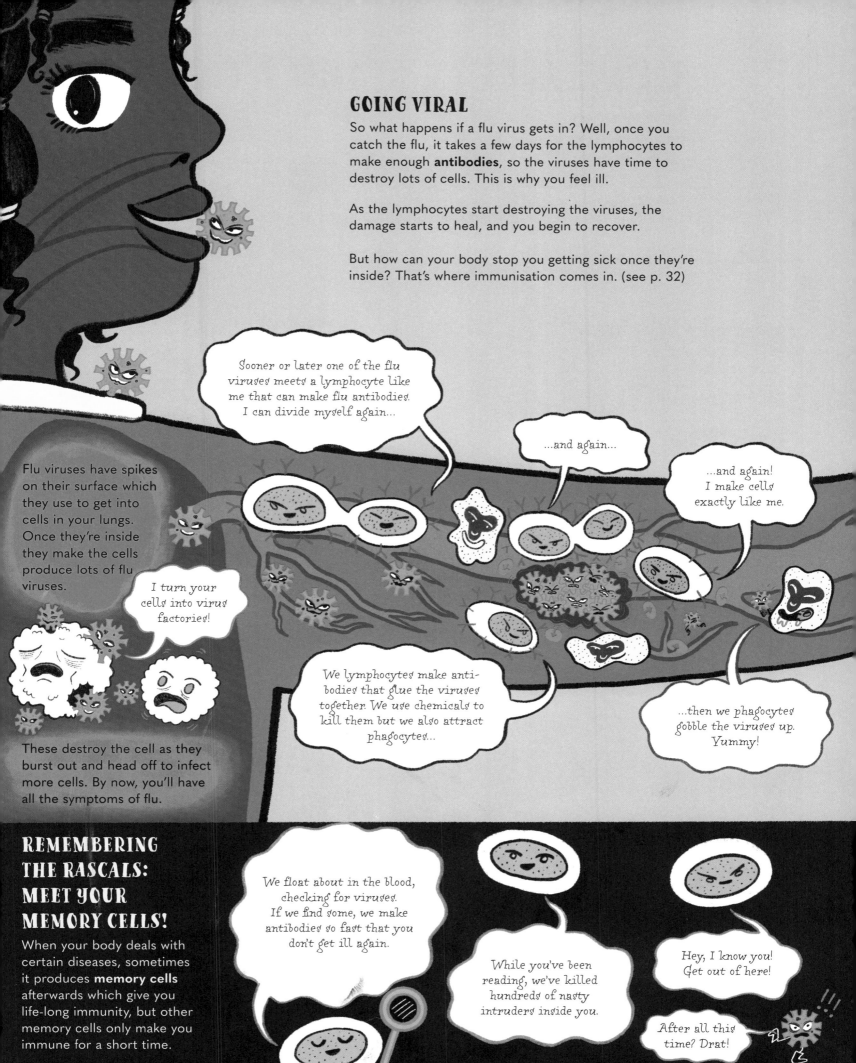

GOING VIRAL

So what happens if a flu virus gets in? Well, once you catch the flu, it takes a few days for the lymphocytes to make enough **antibodies**, so the viruses have time to destroy lots of cells. This is why you feel ill.

As the lymphocytes start destroying the viruses, the damage starts to heal, and you begin to recover.

But how can your body stop you getting sick once they're inside? That's where immunisation comes in. (see p. 32)

Flu viruses have spikes on their surface which they use to get into cells in your lungs. Once they're inside they make the cells produce lots of flu viruses.

These destroy the cell as they burst out and head off to infect more cells. By now, you'll have all the symptoms of flu.

Sooner or later one of the flu viruses meets a lymphocyte like me that can make flu antibodies. I can divide myself again...

...and again...

...and again! I make cells exactly like me.

I turn your cells into virus factories!

We lymphocytes make antibodies that glue the viruses together. We use chemicals to kill them but we also attract phagocytes...

...then we phagocytes gobble the viruses up. Yummy!

REMEMBERING THE RASCALS: MEET YOUR MEMORY CELLS!

When your body deals with certain diseases, sometimes it produces **memory cells** afterwards which give you life-long immunity, but other memory cells only make you immune for a short time.

We float about in the blood, checking for viruses. If we find some, we make antibodies so fast that you don't get ill again.

While you've been reading, we've killed hundreds of nasty intruders inside you.

Hey, I know you! Get out of here!

After all this time? Drat!

HOW VACCINATION WORKS

Immunisation is the effect of a succesful vaccination. It tricks your immune system into making memory cells without you getting ill first. You're injected with a tiny dose of a bacteria or virus that has been killed or weakened. Vaccines cannot hurt you, but they still have antigens, so the immune system leaps into action. Let's try it with measles...

1. You are injected with a weak dose of the measles into your blood.

2. The lymphocytes identify the intruders, make antibodies to fit them and then easily destroy the weakened viruses.

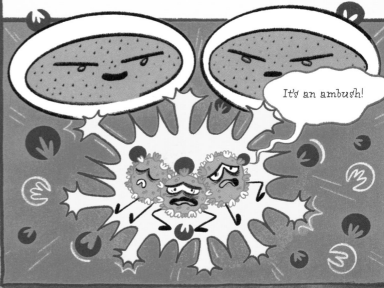

3. The lymphocytes produce memory cells to be ready for the real thing.

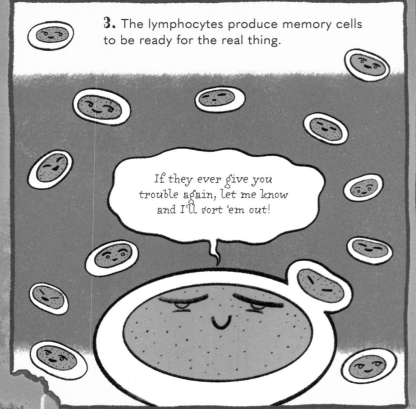

4. Now, if strong measles viruses ever enter your system, the memory cells can get antibodies fired right at them.

Polio (virus)

Tetanus (bacteria)

Measles (virus)

Rubella (virus)

Immunisation programmes now exist in every country in the world, and vaccines have saved millions of lives by protecting us against polio, diphtheria, tetanus, pertussis, measles, the Hib virus, rubella, hepatitis B and more.

Still, we're always on the look-out for the worst offenders!

Hepatitis B (virus)

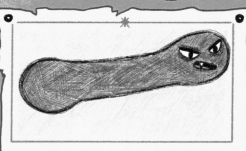

Diphtheria (bacteria)

Pertussis, also known as whooping cough (bacteria)

Hib (*Haemophilus influenzae* type b disease) which causes pneumonia and meningitis (bacteria)

I don't like the look of those!

ANTIVIRALS

Beyond immunisation, we can fight viruses with drugs known as **antivirals**. We only have these for a few viruses so far, but we're ready for flu viruses. The Spanish flu wouldn't be so dangerous today!

You can wash your hands, you can wear your masks, but you'd better get to work if you really want to stop us!

WHAT ABOUT NEW VIRUSES?

For new viruses, like COVID-19 (see p. 20), the effects can be disastrous if it's never infected humans before and spreads rapidly. After all, nobody has memory cells for a new virus, and we certainly don't have vaccines. We can only stave the virus off with antivirals and treatments to help with symptoms while scientists run to the labs!

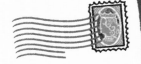

THE MIRACLE DRUG

In 1928, Scottish microbiologist Alexander Fleming went on holiday.
Nice for him, but so what?

Yippee! Two weeks of sun, sea and slimy bacteria!

A FATEFUL VOYAGE

You might have been prescribed **antibiotics** by your doctor if you've been ill: they're drugs that kill bacteria. But how did Alexander's holiday help you recover?

Well, Fleming was experimenting on bacteria that cause sore throats. He grew them on special jelly in glass **Petri dishes**. But he wasn't the tidiest scientist...

A SLIMY SURPRISE

When Professor Fleming went on holiday, he left some of these Petri dishes lying around in his lab. When he got back, he was amazed to discover that a strange green **mould** (a sort of fungus) had started growing all over them.

Well, that's not supposed to happen. Bacteria killed by mould? I need another holiday...

Crumbs, he's back! Everyone hide; he might not spot us...

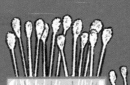

Fleming noticed that the bacteria nearest the mould had vanished and wondered if it had made something that killed the bacteria.

BAC(TERIA) TO WORK!

He grew the mould in liquid and tested the liquid on all sorts of bacteria, quickly discovering that it could kill many types, including some that caused human diseases, by bursting the cell wall that protects them. At last he found the chemical in the liquid that was doing the job, and named it penicillin.

I feel very exposed …

THE END OF PENICILLIN?

Next, he tried injecting mice with penicillin to check it wouldn't harm them. It didn't, but Fleming also found that penicillin didn't work if you kept it for long.

The next step should have been to infect mice with bacteria and see if penicillin would kill them in the animals' bodies, but Fleming never did this, perhaps because it was so difficult to purify and keep penicillin.

For the next ten years it was almost forgotten…

I don't think we're the last mice to ever see that mould!

FLEMING'S WEIRD HOBBY

Bacteria comes in all sorts of different colours. Alexander Fleming collected as many as he could, and used them as paint to make pictures on the jelly he used to grow bacteria.

So unoriginal. Get your own colours, amateur!

THE BACTERIAL BATTLE OF WORLD WAR II

In 1938, two scientists were researching drugs for bacterial infections like tuberculosis (TB), which attacks the lungs and causes fever, weight loss, coughing and even death.

Howard Florey, whose family had suffered from TB, was researching this at Oxford University with Ernst Chain, who was deciding between being a biochemist or pianist. Both men had quick tempers, so work wasn't always easy...

I can't think through all that racket!

I call it the Salmonella Sonata!

Having read Fleming's work, they injected eight mice with harmful bacteria, then gave four of them penicillin...

Ooh, I don't feel well.

Never been better!

NO PENICILLIN

PENICILLIN

All-nighter?

Sure! Nothing else to do.

We're lucky they saved us...

Lucky? They could have killed us!

ENLIST

UK GOES TO WAR

CONTROL – NO PENICILLIN

PENICILLIN

By morning, only the penicillin mice had survived. It worked!

As the Second World War began, there weren't many treatments for soldiers with infected wounds. Even a small one could turn into a fatal abscess or gangrene. Florey and Chain realised that penicillin could save these wounded soldiers' lives.

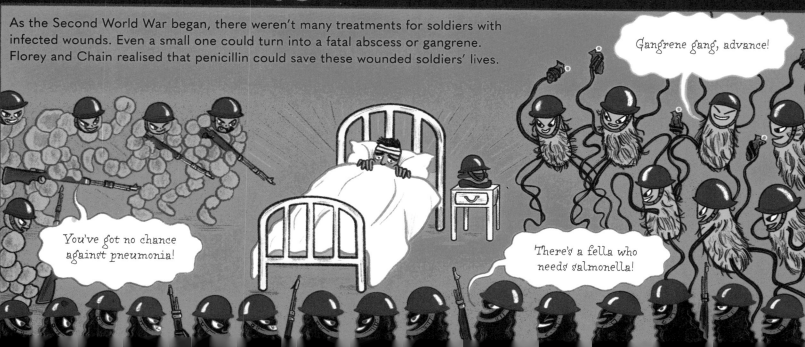

Gangrene gang, advance!

You've got no chance against pneumonia!

There's a fella who needs salmonella!

It took thousands of litres of 'mould juice' for a gram of penicillin, so six 'penicillin girls' tried to speed its growth by testing different growing containers — even hospital bedpans!

Florey wanted to understand how penicillin worked, so he asked Dorothy Hodgkin to investigate. A British chemist and one of the first women to graduate from Oxford with First Class Honours, Hodgkin was a pioneer in **x-ray crystallography**: using x-rays to photograph chemical structures.

Meanwhile, Florey and Chain flew to the US to make penicillin on a bigger scale.

At one point during the Battle of Britain, they soaked their coats in the precious mould to safeguard their work from invasion. Thankfully, they didn't do this when they travelled!

In the US, they searched for a mould that could manufacture penicillin faster, and found one in an old melon! In 1943, mass production began in huge vats of liquor.

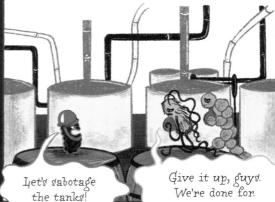

By 1944, near the end of the war, 2.3 million penicillin doses were ready for the Allied landings in France. It saved so many lives that people called it 'the miracle drug of the war'.

Penicillin has saved millions from pneumonia, scarlet fever, meningitis and many respiratory infections. In 1945, Fleming, Florey and Chain won the Nobel Prize in Physiology or Medicine for creating the first widely-available antibiotic.

Meanwhile, Dorothy Hodgkin cracked its structure, opening the door for even more antibiotics, and in 1964 she won the Nobel Prize in Chemistry.

But antibiotics couldn't defeat bacteria completely, and they were about to fight back...

ANTIBIOTIC RESISTANCE

Since penicillin, over one hundred other antibiotics have been discovered, allowing us to treat many diseases and even prevent infection in people with weak immune systems.
But do they work forever?

THE BAD NEWS

Vaccinations, antivirals, antibiotics: so is the show over now? Have we just won the Microbe Wars?

Nope! Since their introduction in the 1940s, we have used antibiotics too much and sometimes for the wrong things, like treating viruses. This leads to **antibiotic resistance**.

This virus is a nightmare; I need antibiotics! The strongest you've got!

Antibiotics won't help you, but some education might!

Maybe I'll prescribe bed-rest and a biology book...

And in some countries they are used on farms, not to treat illness but to make cattle grow faster.

If you give her antibiotics, she'll make it through this food shortage.

My farm can't afford to lose her, but she isn't technically sick. This is tough.

This is great news for bad bacteria, because we're getting resistant to antibiotics! Now this is a fight you'll want to see...

SQUASHING THE SUPERBUGS

Some **superbugs** have to be treated with a few courses of different antibiotics one after another for months — and more are evolving. You can slow this down. Here's how!

- Wash your hands: soap breaks down bacteria by bursting their cell walls

- Don't ask for antibiotics for viruses

- Always take the full course of antibiotics

- Spread the word, not the sickness!

But that's not all! Many more weapons are in the works to take on those pesky bacteria...

WEIRD WEAPONS AGAINST BACTERIA

Scientists are investigating organisms that produce bacteria-killing chemicals, from rainforest plants to marine bacteria.

Sometimes we can strengthen existing antibiotics by changing their structure, but the bacteria might just become resistant again. So what else can we do? Well, scientists are working on all kinds of strange new weapons to combat nasty microbes. Here are some of the most promising projects going on now!

Without antibiotics, they're defenceless! It's just a matter of time until the world is ours!

I'm afraid they've created new weapons, sir, and they're kind of weird...

EAT MORE BACTERIA!

Using antibiotics can kill good bacteria in your gut (see p. 50). Scientists are developing pills of good bacteria to take up space and stop bad ones from settling in!

Sir, we're all booked up. Now shoo!

What a lovely gut-cafe! I think I'll stay forever.

BACTERIAL VACCINES

Immunisation can go beyond viruses. Weakened forms of bad bacteria can ready the immune system to destroy the 'real' ones before they can make you ill.

Who do you work for? What's their plan?

I'll tell you everything, all their secrets!

SNAPP!

SNAPP is a chemical invented to thicken oil and paint. It can rip apart bacteria too, but scientists haven't risked human testing.

WORK IN PROGRESS

This is by far the strangest thing they've ever used against us.

CDOTS

Cdots (carbon dots) are particles activated by light to make chemicals that destroy bacteria. We could use them to make surfaces, disinfectants and antiseptics that kill bacteria if you shine a light on them, or even medicines that kill bacteria inside the body when you shine a special red light on the patient!

QUORUM SENSING INHIBITION (QSI)

Bacteria communicate through chemical signals. This is called quorum sensing and it lets bacteria tell each other where they are and what to do: if there's lots of them in one place, other bacteria should spread out.

Quorum Sensing Inhibition scrambles the signals, so bacteria can't stay organised and may be easier to kill.

WALLABY MILK

The milk that wallabies make contains a chemical 100 times better than penicillin at killing bacteria. Scientists in Australia think it could save us from some superbugs!

PHAGE MEDICINE

Bacteriophages are viruses that infect bacteria. They take over their cells, force the bacteria to make more phages, then kill the bacteria by bursting out of them.

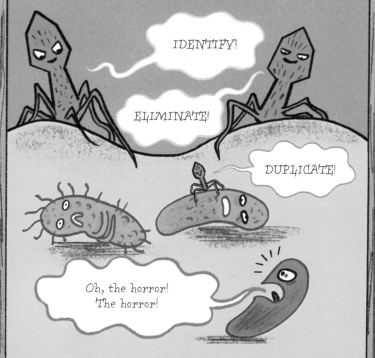

Phages can target specific bacteria without harming others. In Eastern Europe, phage medicine has been used since the 1920s, and it's gaining wider popularity.

They're cheap to produce and easy to find (especially in sewage — they're in your poo!). The hard part is purifying the right one into a pill.

After all that weirdness, how about a snack break? Microbes can certainly help with that!

YUMMY MICROBES!

If we only talk about diseases, you'd want to avoid microbes completely. Actually, most of them are harmless or helpful, and without them we wouldn't have some of your favourite foods.

YOGHURT AND CHEESE

Bacteria and moulds are essential for cheese and yoghurt. They convert sugars and proteins into tastier chemicals.

MEAT-FREE MEAT

Fusarium fungus can be grown, harvested and processed into high-protein foods that look, smell, and taste meaty, with no animals involved!

42

FERMENTED FOODS

Foods like yoghurt can have a slightly sour or fizzy taste, because they've been fermented for a while by busy microbes.

> We all help make fermented foods like miso, kimchi, sauerkraut and kefir.

Miso is a savoury Japanese ingredient made from soy beans.

Kimchi is Korean, and made from pickling vegetables. In many other countries, 'kimchi' refers to spicy pickled cabbage.

Kefir is a fermented milk drink like thin yoghurt, from Eastern Europe and Asia.

Sauerkraut, from Germany, is fermented cabbage.

BREAD AND ALCOHOL

Without microbes there would only be flat bread, and no alcohol. **Yeast** is a fungus that has been used for baking and brewing for thousands of years.

> Mix us with flour and water, I'll eat the flour's sugar to reproduce, then we'll make some alcohol and carbon dioxide. Bake us up and you've got bread!

> Fellas, we're not getting out of this alive, but we'll make a lovely loaf.

> We're the real bakers. The name's Saccharomyces; or yeast for short.

RIP

RIP

But if there's alcohol in bread, why doesn't it make you drunk?

Well, there's not much alcohol in the dough by the time it's risen, and it all evaporates in the oven.

> To make stronger drinks like gin, whisky and vodka, you have to concentrate the alcohol by removing some of the water.

> If you mix me with sugary grape juice I'll grow and reproduce, making carbon dioxide and lots of alcohol for fizzy beer, wine and cider.

43

YOUR MICROBE FRIENDS

Microbes don't just help us with food. All sorts of bacteria and fungi are busy behind the scenes, assisting us in ways we rarely think about. Welcome to the wonderful world of microbe workers...

MICROBE LAUNDRIES

Bacteria make **enzymes** to break down chemicals in their cells. Enzymes work best at the bacteria's natural living temperature: usually under 50 degrees Celsius. We use enzymes in biological washing powders and liquids to attack stains, because they clean clothes at low temperatures, saving energy.

Good grief! What have they been doing?

MICROBE CLEANERS

Bacteria can even clean up pollution from oil spills and harmful metals like lead and uranium. Bacteria helped clean up polluted soil from the old chemical works and oil refineries on the building site for the 2012 London Olympics complex.

When do we get our medals?

A country full of fields, and they want to play here!

SEWAGE

YUCK ALERT! Bacteria clean up sewage from factories and houses, including from your shower, washing machine and toilet.

Methane is used to fuel the plant, and the leftover sludge gets dried out for fertiliser.

The sewage goes into a tank and all the solids sink. We break the solids down to make methane gas.

MICROBE DRUG FACTORIES

DIABETES

Your blood carries sugar to feed your cells. They're always hungry, so there needs to be a steady level (known as a concentration) of sugar in your blood. But surely you'd have lots of sugar in your blood right after a meal, and hardly any at night?

That's why your pancreas makes **insulin**. Insulin tells your body to remove excess glucose from your blood for storage in your liver and muscles.

Some people can't produce insulin. This condition is called type 1 diabetes. Without insulin treatment, it can cause sight loss, heart disease, kidney and nerve damage, and sometimes death. Until the 1920s, the only treatment was a dangerously strict diet.

Now, human DNA containing the recipe for insulin is given to microbes, and they make it for us! In the 1980s, it was taken from the pancreas of cows or pigs, but now we can make it in clean factories.

> *It's purer than animal insulin, with no risk of disease.*

> *Human DNA gives us the recipe, and E. Coli bacteria and yeast mix it up!*

> *We're grown in tanks to make loads really fast!*

MICROBE FACTORY HALL OF FAME

Interleukin-2 can treat some cancers.

Interferon beta-1b can combat multiple sclerosis.

Human growth hormone helps children with growing problems.

Keratinocyte growth factor guards cancer patients' cells during chemotherapy.

> *The liquid pours into a filter bed. We sit on the stones and break any nasty chemicals into harmless water and carbon dioxide.*

> *Now it can safely run into a river, clean enough to drink!*

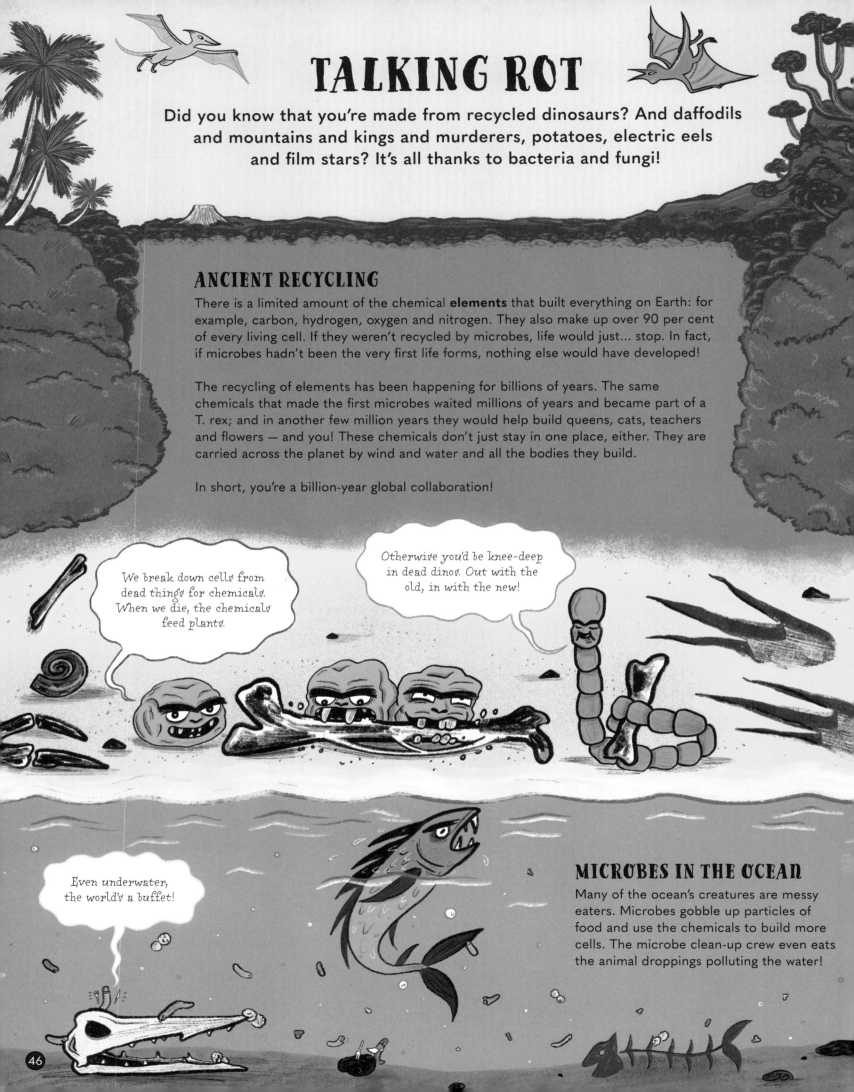

TALKING ROT

Did you know that you're made from recycled dinosaurs? And daffodils and mountains and kings and murderers, potatoes, electric eels and film stars? It's all thanks to bacteria and fungi!

ANCIENT RECYCLING

There is a limited amount of the chemical **elements** that built everything on Earth: for example, carbon, hydrogen, oxygen and nitrogen. They also make up over 90 per cent of every living cell. If they weren't recycled by microbes, life would just... stop. In fact, if microbes hadn't been the very first life forms, nothing else would have developed!

The recycling of elements has been happening for billions of years. The same chemicals that made the first microbes waited millions of years and became part of a T. rex; and in another few million years they would help build queens, cats, teachers and flowers — and you! These chemicals don't just stay in one place, either. They are carried across the planet by wind and water and all the bodies they build.

In short, you're a billion-year global collaboration!

We break down cells from dead things for chemicals. When we die, the chemicals feed plants.

Otherwise you'd be knee-deep in dead dinos. Out with the old, in with the new!

Even underwater, the world's a buffet!

MICROBES IN THE OCEAN

Many of the ocean's creatures are messy eaters. Microbes gobble up particles of food and use the chemicals to build more cells. The microbe clean-up crew even eats the animal droppings polluting the water!

MICROBES IN THE FOREST

Many trees shed their leaves in winter. Imagine how deep the piles would get if they didn't rot away! The trees would starve and die, because the chemicals in their old leaves wouldn't go back into the soil for them to use for *new* leaves.

If the trees died, so would the insects that eat from them!

And the birds that eat the insects!

And the animals that eat the birds!

Nitrogen in, fertiliser out!

MICROBES ON THE FARM

Plants like peas, beans and clover have lumps on their roots called root nodules. They're full of bacteria that take nitrogen from the air and turn it into **fertiliser**.

Other plants have to get their nitrogen from soil, and when there isn't enough, farmers have to add chemical fertilisers, or they can grow clover and plough it in!

Who needs oxygen when you can make acid? It preserves the grass, and it's full of vitamins!

LINEN

Flax crop stems make linen thread. The fibres are all stuck together inside the stems though, so they're 'ungummed' by bacteria or fungi rotting them in water.

SILAGE

When there isn't enough grass for animals to eat, farmers feed them silage — *pickled* grass! It's chopped up, squished down and covered to keep out oxygen, then grass bacteria get to work fermenting.

We break down a gluey protein called pectin. If you've made jam, pectin helped it set.

Bet you thought decomposition was gross. Fertiliser, food, fabric: we're rotters and proud!

FARMYARD RUMINATIONS

There are lots of large animals, including giraffes, antelope, sheep and cattle that survive on grass or other leaves. How do they do it? Well, they don't — not on their own. These animals are called **ruminants**, and ruminants all have multiple stomach chambers with huge farms inside. No, that's not the wrong way around. A ruminant's gut is a microbe farm!

It's a perfectly natural rabbit habit! I've seen you biting your nails.

Here it comes again...

JUST DROPPING IN FOR A BITE

Rabbits aren't ruminants because they only have one stomach chamber, but they're a good introduction to internal microbe farms. Rabbits have theirs near the end of the gut, beyond the bit that absorbs nutrients. So what's their secret?

YUCK ALERT! Rabbits eat their own droppings, so the food goes through their gut twice, and second time around they can absorb the nutrients released by the microbes.

We're not talking about the hard, black droppings. Those come second. Their first ones just look like chewed grass, and the rabbits like to eat them privately in their burrows (I'm sure you would too...). Other animals, including chimpanzees and gorillas, sometimes do the same thing.

JOURNEY TO THE CENTRE OF THE COW

Cows are proper ruminants! Their stomachs have four chambers, and the largest one — the rumen — can hold over 180 litres of grass and water: that's more than a bathful!

It also holds billions of microbes, which break down the grass and release its nutrients. The nutrients get into the blood farther down the gut, along with millions of digested microbes, but they reproduce so fast there are always plenty more.

When a cow eats grass, it goes into the rumen for digestion. After a while, the cow sits down, brings the half-digested grass back up into its mouth, and gives it a good long chew to mash it up with saliva and make it easier for the microbes to finish digesting it. This is called 'chewing the cud'!

Digesting grass like this makes us burp methane, a gas which hurts the climate.

Mooriel over there can burp 500 litres a day: she's an ecological menace!

Methane gas is only produced by a few rogue microbes, so scientists are looking for ways to target them.

One way is to feed cows with food that those microbes don't like, or maybe even vaccinate them!

What's for lunch? I hope it's grass. I love grass.

If we give her more nutrients, she'll give us more grass!

Ah, this is the life: breaking down mulch in an old cow's stomach.

YOUR PERSONAL MICROBES

Your body is made of 30 trillion cells, but there are just as many microbes on you too, and probably 10 trillion more! They're called your microbiome. They're all over your skin (10,000,000 per square centimetre) and your gut is full of them. You wash away most of the skin ones when you shower, but you're soon covered again — and that's a good thing!

Open the flood gates!

We can live on the skin, eyeballs, nose, mouth, gut and genitalia. You'll even find some of us swimming around in the blood.

Your gut microbiome has trillions of microbes, weighing a whole kilogram in an adult, mostly in the large intestine (bowel).

EYES

We think that *Corynebacterium mastitidis* stimulates cells in the eye to release chemicals into our tears that kill harmful bacteria that can cause blindness.

MOUTH

Streptococcus salivarius may help stop bad breath by growing more successfully than the stinky bacteria.

Where did THEY come from?

VAGINA

Lactobacillus (the same bacteria used in yoghurt!) keep the vagina slightly acidic, which prevents most bacteria from growing there. When a baby is born through here, it picks up some of the lactobacillus, which help it digest milk.

TURF WARS

Some microbes can only live in your warm and sweaty armpits. Others prefer the oils in your face, and some grow best on the dry deserts of your arms and legs. Most are harmless — in fact, they take up so much space that there's less room for any bad ones!

But when bad ones turn up, the good ones can warn you. For instance, they might tell your skin cells to make proteins that kill the harmful microbes, but they also prevent your immune system from reacting too strongly and hurting you too.

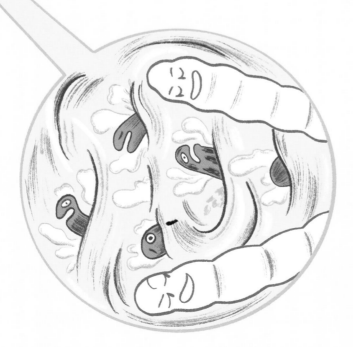

WASTE NOT, WANT NOT

Doctors are starting to use gut bacteria to treat some conditions with poo transplants!

Generally, the more types you have, the better, and some of them leave in your poo — or **faeces,** as scientists call it. People with gut conditions are often missing some of the helpful ones. With a *faecal microbial transplant,* many of these conditions improve. This means putting poo from someone with a strong microbiome into the patient's gut.

Who knows, maybe eventually there'll be faecal donation centres as well as blood donation centres...?

THE LIVING GUT

You might have noticed that you feel a bit unwell after a course of antibiotics. This is because some antibiotics kill part of the gut microbiome, and you won't feel 100 per cent better until you replace them. Yoghurt can do the trick. It's full of lactobacillus!

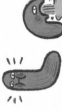

HOW TO TALK TO MICROBES

So, you have microbes that help you and an immune system that helps you, but how do they work together? And if your immune system is always hunting for strange cells, why doesn't it destroy all of your gut microbes?

FANCY A CHAT?

Amazingly, when you're a tiny baby, your gut microbes teach your immune system to ignore them by using **chemical chat**: they create special chemicals to make immune cells react as though the bacteria are actually part of *you*.

Now, take a little bit, and say what you would do to microbes like me?

GOOD!

BAD

Attack! Wait... No... Accept!

FRIENDS NOT FOES

I'm trying to help you!

Some illnesses, like Crohn's disease or type 1 diabetes, are caused by your immune system getting confused and attacking you. Scientists think that in most people, bacterial chemical chat teaches the immune system not to do this.

Get him, lads; he's talking nonsense!

BATTLE ORDERS!

If harmful microbes invade your gut, your microbe army uses chemical chat to tell your gut wall to make chemicals to defend itself. And of course, because the good microbes are already there, there isn't much room for the bad ones to settle down.

But the bad ones can be sneaky. We've now discovered that bad bacteria can also use chemical chat to escape the immune system, for instance by increasing the level of harmful chemicals they release.

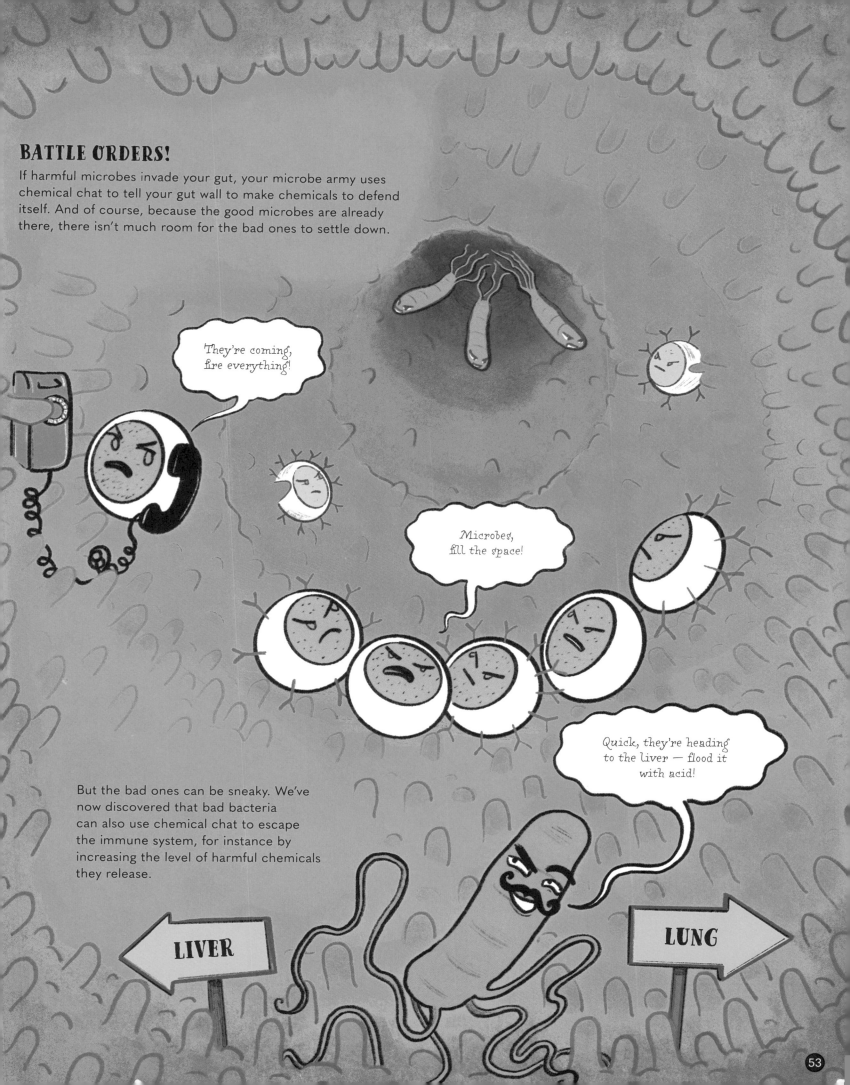

RAISING YOUR ARMY

By now, you can see how important your microbe army is.
But where do they come from? And beyond what they can do for you,
what can you do for them?

FIRST RECRUITS

You start recruiting microbe soldiers before you are even born! You pick up microbes inside the womb, and more from the birth canal when it's time to move out. But what if you're born by caesarean section, when a surgeon lifts you out through the belly?

Well, you pick up microbes from your mum's skin instead. These microbes develop best if a baby is fed with breast milk because of its helpful bacteria and nourishing chemicals, instead of formula milk from a bottle.

GATHERING YOUR FORCES

Once you are a bit older, your diet makes a *huge* difference to how many and what type of microbes live in your gut. You also swap microbes with other people in your house, with your pets, and even with the dust in your house — everything is clamouring for a place on you, your house, and your pets! Your microbes also vary depending on what country you live in and whether you live in a city or in the countryside.

BOOT CAMP: STRENGTHEN YOUR SOLDIERS!

Eat lots of vegetables. The chemicals in plants reach your microbes without being digested as much as meat, so there's more for your microbes to use!

Feed your army! **Prebiotics** are compounds in food that go straight to your microbes!

Avoid processed, sugary and fatty foods. They don't have enough nutrients for you and your microbes.

Eat an army! **Probiotics** are foods that contain good microbes. Common probiotics include yoghurt, kefir, miso, sauerkraut and some cheeses.

Don't be *too* clean. If you always scrub everything with anti-bacterial disinfectants, you'll destroy lots of microbes that keep you healthy.

Eat plenty of fibre. You can't digest it, but your microbes *love* it.

MICROBE PARADE! WHO'S THE BEST?

People in Western countries tend to eat higher amounts of processed foods and meat and fewer plants than people elsewhere. Their microbes are starving for nutrients!

The Hadza people in Tanzania have the biggest, best microbe armies in the world. The Hadza forage for wild plants and honey and hunt their own meat. Their diet varies with the seasons, so they eat a huge range of nutritious plants.

BEYOND THE BATTLEFIELD

So we know microbes can be soldiers, teachers and doctors in your body, but here are some more jobs they do that we're only just beginning to understand!

You eat the good stuff, and I'll take it from there!

NUTRITIONISTS

Microbes help to regulate your weight. Fat and thin mice have different microbes in their guts and it seems that this is also true of humans. Perhaps in future there will be pills full of microbes to help control weight!

Oh dear, have they fallen over again?

Double dose of K, please!

CHEMISTS

Microbes also make vitamins that you need to function properly, including B vitamins, vitamin K and folic acid. You need B vitamins to release energy from food and to keep many of your tissues healthy. Vitamin K helps your blood clot, and folic acid makes red blood cells and helps babies' spinal cords to develop properly.

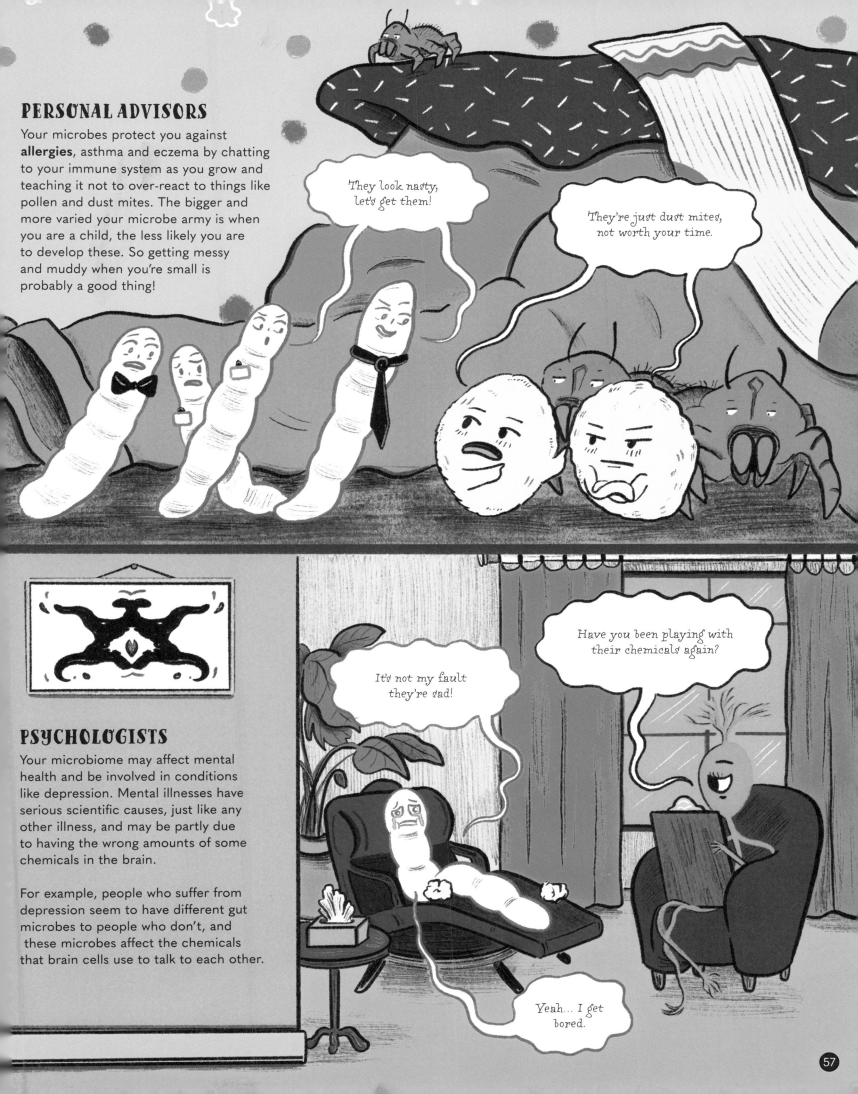

PERSONAL ADVISORS

Your microbes protect you against **allergies**, asthma and eczema by chatting to your immune system as you grow and teaching it not to over-react to things like pollen and dust mites. The bigger and more varied your microbe army is when you are a child, the less likely you are to develop these. So getting messy and muddy when you're small is probably a good thing!

PSYCHOLOGISTS

Your microbiome may affect mental health and be involved in conditions like depression. Mental illnesses have serious scientific causes, just like any other illness, and may be partly due to having the wrong amounts of some chemicals in the brain.

For example, people who suffer from depression seem to have different gut microbes to people who don't, and these microbes affect the chemicals that brain cells use to talk to each other.

THE END?

The Microbe Wars will certainly keep going through your lifetime. What's likely to happen next?

COMING SOON:

BACTERIA STRIKE BACK

More bacteria will become resistant to antibiotics. We'll have to be much more careful using them or curable diseases may become untreatable, and surgery will carry bigger infection risks. With any luck, new antibiotics will be found. But don't count on it.

OUR BEST DEFENCE

We may develop vaccines against more diseases. A promising malaria vaccine is being tested now.

DOUBLE AGENTS

We will understand more about beneficial microbes fighting on our side, and how we can help them to help us.

THE SECRET WEAPON

We may find ways to kill harmful bacteria that don't involve antibiotics: phages, wallabies, Cdots... Who knows what we might find next? Some of these ideas have come from very unlikely sources.

BUG HUNT

We may find better ways to kill the insects that pass on harmful microbes, but we need to avoid killing harmless or helpful insects at the same time.

YOUR PART TO PLAY

Most people don't know about the amazing world of microbes, but now *you* do. You know some of the history of the Microbe Wars and the scientists and medics who have discovered the weapons we use to fight them.

You know microbes are almost everywhere, although most of them are invisible to us. You know they rot food, but also help make it. You know that they can cause disease, but also cure it. You know that we all live with microbes all the time — we even share our bodies with them.

You know that most of them are on our side.

But the Microbe Wars will go on and on, and now it's *your* turn to join the fight.

How? By telling everyone you know about the amazing world of microbes!

GLOSSARY

A host of handy terms. Reckon you could learn them all?

Algae: microbes which make their food by photosynthesis

Allergy: an over-reaction by the immune system to an antigen

Amoeba: a shape-changing microbe that lives in water

Anaesthetic: a medical chemical used to numb part of the body or put you to sleep

Antibiotics: chemicals produced by fungi to destroy bacteria

Antibiotic resistance: when a microbe has lost its vulnerability to one or more antibiotics

Antibodies: proteins produced by certain white blood cells to destroy bacteria and viruses

Antigens: molecules on cell and virus surfaces that identify what they are

Antiseptic: a substance or process that destroys microbes on living things

Antivirals: drugs used to treat illness caused by viruses

Aseptic: very clean; free from microbes

Bacteria: simple single-celled microbes

Bacteriophage: a virus that infects bacteria, often just called a 'phage'

Bifidobacterium: a helpful bacteria found in the human gut

Buboes: painful lumps in the armpits and groin caused by plague

Chemical chat: how bacteria communicate using chemical signals

Coronavirus: a virus named for the surface spikes that resemble a crown

DNA: chemical instructions for making a living thing

Elements: chemicals that cannot be broken down into a simpler substance

Enzyme: substance produced by cells to speed up chemical reactions

Faeces: the scientific name for poo

Fermentation: microbes breaking down sugars to use as food, without using oxygen

Fertiliser: substances added to soil to improve the growth of plants

Fungi: a group of organisms which use liquid to break down the cells of other organisms

Immunisation: making someone immune to a disease, usually by giving them a vaccine

Innoculation: putting a potentially harmful substance into the body to prompt immunisation

Infection: the act of passing on an illness caused by a microbe

Insulin: a chemical produced by the body to help control blood glucose levels

Lymphocyte: a white blood cell that makes antibodies

Memory cells: long-lived immune cells that can remember invasive antigens

Microbe: a microscopic organism, often single-celled but sometimes multicellular

Microbiome: the community of microbes that live on and in another organism

Moulds: microscopic fungi that grow as long threads

Mutation: a change in DNA or RNA instructions

Organism: a living thing

Outbreak: a sudden increase in disease cases in a particular area

Pasteurisation: heating foods to destroy the microbes inside them

Petri dish: glass dish often used to grow bacteria and fungi in laboratories

Phagocyte: a type of white blood cell that breaks down bacteria and viruses

Photosynthesis: how plants make sugar using water, carbon dioxide and sunlight

Prebiotics: foods that humans can't digest, but that gut microbes can use

Probiotics: foods that contain live, helpful microbes

Protist: a group of microbes found in soil and water

Protozoa: protists which are like tiny animals

Pus: a bodily fluid containing dead white blood cells and bacteria

Quorum Sensing Inhibition (QSI): interfering with how bacteria chemically communicate

Quarantine: a period of isolation to prevent the spread of infectious disease

RNA: chemical instructions used by some viruses instead of DNA

Ruminant: an animal that brings up food from its stomach to chew again

Spore: a reproductive cell made by many types of microbe

Superbugs: bacteria that are resistant to many antibiotics

Toxin: a substance which is harmful if it gets into the body

Vaccine: a substance that makes the body immune to a disease

Virus: a microbe that infects living cells and reproduces inside them

X-ray crystallography: using x-rays to work out the structure of chemicals

Yeast: a microscopic fungus used in brewing and baking

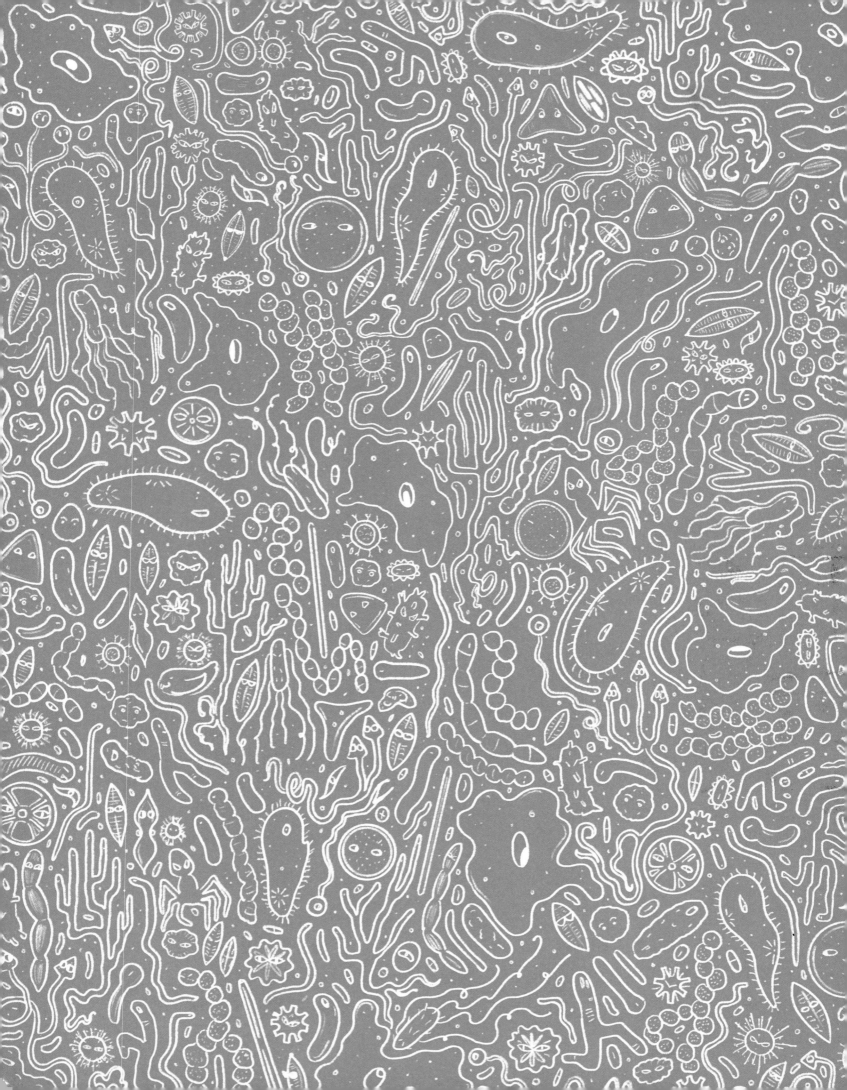